Foreword

Hinduism is the world's most ancient living religion. It is practiced by over 80 percent of India's one billion people as well as many other people in countries throughout the world. The original name for Hinduism is Sanatana Dharma, or the eternal religion. The word *Hindu* came from *Sindhu*, the Sanskrit word for the river Indus.

Hinduism is based on the ancient scriptures called the Vedas. It teaches that God is one but his names and forms are many. God is the soul of the universe and also the inmost soul in every human heart. The ultimate goal of life is to know God, and love all people because of God's presence within them. A Hindu often chooses one particular form of God for worship and regards other forms as expressions of the same God. Freedom of worship is the most basic freedom for Hindus.

Temples play a vital role in Hinduism. They are centers of learning, places of pilgrimage, and shrines of worship. For a Hindu, the temple is the external symbol of the real temple in the human heart. The deity on the temple altar reminds a Hindu of the shrine in our heart where God dwells as our inmost soul. The offerings of fruits, flowers, and other special items to God symbolize the real offerings of our prayerful thoughts. A Hindu feels the presence of God in the temple and firmly believes that God never abandons his devotees.

This book by Dr. Mahendra Jani and Dr. Vandana Jani is an excellent presentation of Hindu temples and Hindu religious practices.

Swami Adiswarananda
Minister and Spiritual Leader,
Ramakrishna-Vivekananda Center of New York

Books in the Series

What You Will See Inside…

- *A Catholic Church*

- *Lo que se puede ver dentro de una iglesia católica*

- *A Hindu Temple*

- *A Mosque*

- *A Synagogue*

What You Will See Inside

See Inside

A HINDU TEMPLE

Dr. Mahendra Jani
and Dr. Vandana Jani
with Photographs by Neirah Bhargava
and Vijay Dave

Walking Together, Finding the Way
SKYLIGHT PATHS®
PUBLISHING
Woodstock, Vermont

What You Will See Inside a Hindu Temple

2005 First Printing
Text © 2005 Dr. Mahendra Jani and Dr. Vandana Jani
Photos © 2005 Neirah Bhargava and Vijay Dave

For information regarding permission to reprint material from this book, please mail or fax your request in writing to SkyLight Paths Publishing, Permissions Department, at the address / fax number listed below, or send an e-mail to permissions@skylightpaths.com.

The authors would like to dedicate this book to the children of Vivekananda Vidyapith, Wayne, New Jersey, who remained a constant source of inspiration, unbounded love and joy for over thirty years.

The authors would like to thank Mytheli Sreenivas, Pranav Jani, Uma Ramakrishna, K. Prasad, and Rakesh Bhargava for their valuable suggestions and help. They would also like to extend their special thanks to Revered Swami Adiswarananda, minister and spiritual leader, Ramakrishna Vivekananda Center of New York, for his inspiration and encouragement to write this book.

Grateful acknowledgment is given to the following institutions for their generosity to allow us to take photographs inside their temples and for giving permission to reprint their photographs: Shree Sanatan Mandir, Parsippany, New Jersey (cover—student offering flowers, p. 7 *murtis,* p. 8 *shivalingam,* p. 11 *abhishekam,* p. 12 *arati);* Connecticut Valley Hindu Temple Society, Middletown, Connecticut (p. 5 bell, p. 6 shrine, p. 9 deities, p. 30 temple); BAPS Swaminarayan Sanstha, Shri Swaminarayan Mandirs of USA (cover—top of temple, p. 3 *shikhar* and pillars, p. 5 temple, p. 23 *annakuta,* p. 30 temple); Arya Samaj of Bergen County, Ridgewood, New Jersey (p. 15 *homa);* Hindu Samaj and Cultural Center, Wappingers Falls, New York; Vivekananda Vidyapith, Wayne, New Jersey (cover—student meditating, front flap—students greeting, pp. 3 and 31 *namaste,* pp. 16 and 17 books and library, pp. 18 and 19 chanting in prayer hall, learning Sanskrit and food drive, p. 24 shrine); Hindu Temple and Cultural Society of USA, Bridgewater, New Jersey (p. 30 temple). Thanks also to the following individuals who provided photographs to reprint in the book: Shyam Kumari Bhargava (p. 22 three food plates); S. Sivakumar (p. 26 Vidyarambha); R. Krishnan (p. 26 Upanayana); Gayatri and Shrey Desai (p. 27 Vivaha); Mihir Shah (p. 28 family shrine); V. Sreenivas (p. 29 entering a new home).

Library of Congress Cataloging-in-Publication Data
Jani, Mahendra.
What you will see inside a Hindu temple / Mahendra Jani and Vandana Jani ; with photographs by Neirah Bhargava and Vijay Dave.
p. cm. — (What you will see inside—)
ISBN 1-59473-116-0
1. Temples, Hindu—Juvenile literature. 2. Temples, Hindu—Pictorial works. I. Jani, Vandana, 1946–   . II. Bhargava, Neirah. III. Dave, Vijay. IV. Title. V. Series.
BL1243.74.J36 2005
294.5'35—dc22

2005020962

10 9 8 7 6 5 4 3 2 1

Manufactured in China

SkyLight Paths Publishing is creating a place where people of different spiritual traditions come together for challenge and inspiration, a place where we can help each other understand the mystery that lies at the heart of our existence.

SkyLight Paths sees both believers and seekers as a community that increasingly transcends traditional boundaries of religion and denomination—people wanting to learn from each other, *walking together, finding the way.*

Book and Jacket Design: Dawn DeVries Sokol with Tim Holtz and Jenny Buono

SkyLight Paths, "Walking Together, Finding the Way" and colophon are trademarks of LongHill Partners, Inc. registered in the U.S. Patent and Trademark Office.

Walking Together, Finding the Way
Published by SkyLight Paths Publishing
A Division of LongHill Partners, Inc.
Sunset Farm Offices, Route 4, P.O. Box 237
Woodstock, VT 05091
Tel: (802) 457-4000   Fax: (802) 457-4004
www.skylightpaths.com

Welcome! *Namaste!*

NAMASTE!* is a greeting in Sanskrit, the ancient holy language for Hindus. It means, "I salute God within you." Hindus believe that the God who created the sun, the moon, the planets, the earth, and all of us is the same God who lives in our hearts. When we say *Namaste*, we are honoring God who dwells within all of us.

God is everywhere, and God easily can be found in good people and in temples where God is worshiped by devotees. People who come to pray in the temple are called "devotees" because they are devoted to God.

The Hindu religion began in India. Today, Hindus—who live in every country in the world—consider India their holy place. To worship God and be good citizens, Hindus build temples wherever they live. Hindu temples are called by various names such as *mandir,** *devalaya,* and *devasthana.** All these words mean that a temple is God's dwelling place.

Some temples are small; some are big. Some temples are simple on the outside, and others have beautiful carvings on the walls and pillars. The top of a temple, called the *shikhar,** can be rounded or pointed. On the *shikhar* there is a *kalasha,** a round pitcher-like brass or golden crown. It catches the first rays of the sun and reflects light all around. Some temples also have a flag or banner on top to remind us that God is more important than anything else in the world. The flag waving with the wind invites people of all faiths to come to the temple.

So, come inside a Hindu temple and enjoy the presence of God and the company of faithful devotees.

*When you see this mark (*), look at the bottom of the page to see how the Sanskrit word is pronounced.

Namaste: nah-mas-TAY
Mandir: mun-DEER
Devasthana: deh-va-STAN

Shikhar: shih-KAHR
Kalasha: kah-LA-sha

A Visit to God

ON WEEKENDS and special celebration days, a Hindu temple is bustling, lively, and filled with people. Some devotees also go to a temple on weekdays, in the mornings or evenings. We believe that going to a temple is like paying a visit to God. We use a special Sanskrit word, *darshan*, for seeing God in the temple. Just as we prepare ourselves when we visit someone we love and respect, we make special preparations before visiting God.

OFFERINGS: People bring offerings to the temple. Some men wear traditional Indian *dhotis,** while women wear *saris.**

When we go to a temple, we must be clean and pure. By keeping our bodies clean, we remember to keep our minds pure. We take a shower or bath at home and wear clean clothes, or clothes kept just for temple visits. At special celebrations, most people wear new outfits.

It is a tradition to take with us some offerings to God, which may be flowers, fruits, whole coconuts, sweets, milk, and money. However, it is not what someone brings that is important. In the Bhagavad Gita,* a holy book of Hindus, Lord Krishna says, "Whatever a devotee offers with love, may it be a flower, a leaf, or even water, I accept and enjoy."

We carry the offerings respectfully and do not put them on the ground or let them touch our feet or shoes. We do not even sniff the flowers we carry or taste the food. Before entering the temple, we take off our shoes so that we do not carry dirt inside. Then we wash our hands. Now we are ready to enter into God's dwelling place.

FLOWERS: Hindu temples are filled with bright flower offerings.

Dhotis: DOH-tees   *Saris:* SAH-rees   Bhagavad Gita: bah-ga-VAD GHEE-tah

We enter the temple by first putting our right foot inside the door. This shows that we are entering with the right frame of mind. Near the entrance we may find hanging brass bells. We gently ring the bells to announce our presence to God and focus our minds on God.

BELLS: Temple bells help us focus our minds on God, driving away all other thoughts as the sound of a bell drives away all other sounds.

Beginning with *Om*

AS WE ENTER THE TEMPLE, we may see the symbol *Om**
written on the door. Hindus believe the sound of *Om*
was the first creation of God. It is a sacred syllable made
from the three sounds A-U-M. We worship *Om* as a uni-
versal symbol for the One God. All Hindu prayers begin
with *Om*.

Hindus believe that there is only one God. This God is infinite,
which means that God is everywhere and always has been and
always will be. Hindus refer to this One Infinite God as Brahman.

OM: The Sanskrit symbol for *Om.* The
sound of *Om* was the first creation of
God, and it begins all Hindu prayers.

In ancient times in India, Hindus worshiped Brahman through
fire. Over time, many other forms of the One God have been introduced. Just as water
is called by many different names and appears in many forms—ice, snow, plain water,
and steam—the One God is called by many names and has many forms. These forms
are referred to as gods and goddesses. Hindus may worship any form of God that has
special meaning for them. God can be worshiped as both father and mother.

Hindus believe that the One God has three characteristics that form a trinity of
gods—Brahma, Vishnu, and Shiva (or Maheshwara*). Brahma creates the world,
Vishnu preserves it, and Shiva destroys it in order to create it again.

When we enter a Hindu temple, we will see one main shrine and many small
shrines. A shrine is an area where the images of God, called *murtis,** are placed. The
word *murta* means "one who has a
body." God is believed to be living in
these *murtis.* In some temples, we
may find all *murtis* together in one
shrine. The *murtis* are decorated with
colorful handmade clothes, beautiful
ornaments, and garlands of flowers.

Om: ohm
Maheshwara: ma-HEY-shwa-ra
Murtis: MOOR-tees

MURTIS: Beautiful clothes are made for the images of God, called
murtis, in which God comes to live and be worshiped.

One God, Many Forms

WHEN WE VISIT A TEMPLE WE WILL SEE MANY FORMS OF GOD. Each form expresses special powers and virtues. Hindu children learn stories about each form of God when they are very young and develop special love for one or more forms. They also learn hymns and songs for each form of God. People love to sing these in the temple.

Lord Vishnu means "all pervading"—he is always with us, everywhere, and is the preserver. Vishnu is also known as Lord Narayana.* He holds a conch shell (a symbol of the sound of *Om*), a discus (a symbol of time), a mace (a symbol of protection), and a lotus (a symbol of purity); his several hands show the divine power of God.

Lord Shiva likes to meditate and is compassionate to all. If people pray to him sincerely, he fulfills their wishes, ignoring their weaknesses. Lord Shiva is a great dancer, and his dancing *murti,* known as Nataraj,* is worshiped in many temples. Lord Shiva is also worshiped symbolically as a *shivalingam,* a special smooth kind of marble found in nature.

Lord Ganesha* helps us by removing all obstacles on our way to spiritual growth. That is why he is worshiped first in all temples and in every ritual. His big elephant head tells us that he is intelligent, has keen powers of observation, and is very good at listening.

Lord Rama is often seen with his wife, the goddess Sita. Their lives, described in the great poem *Ramayana*,* inspire people to love and respect family members and all others. You will see Lord Rama, Mother Sita, Rama's younger brother Lakshmana, and their devoted servant Hanumana worshiped together in a temple. Because of Hanumana's fearlessness and single-minded devotion to Rama and Sita, he too is worshiped as God.

Lord Krishna is worshiped in different forms. He is worshiped as Baby Krishna; as a young man dancing with his cow-herd friends or standing alone, leaning on a tree and playing the flute; and as the charioteer and guide of his friend Arjuna on the battlefield. He is also seen as a mighty warrior. His teaching to Arjuna is known as Bhagavad Gita (the song of God), one of the greatest of all Hindu scriptures.

SHIVALINGAM: A legend says that in order to show the mighty power of God, Lord Shiva appeared as an infinite pillar of fire in front of Lord Vishnu and Lord Brahma. *Shivalingam,* a smooth kind of marble, is the symbol of that fire pillar.

BABY KRISHNA: Baby Krishna is shown enjoying butter offered by loving devotees.

LORD KRISHNA AND HIS FRIEND ARJUNA: Lord Krishna driving the chariot of Arjuna on the battlefield.

Lord Venkateswara (Balagi), a form of Lord Narayana

Lakshmana, Lord Rama, Mother Sita, and devoted servant Hanumana

Lord Nataraj

Lord Ganesha

God is also worshiped as Mother of the Universe. She is a loving and compassionate mother, but also strong and powerful in order to protect her children. Some of the forms of the Mother of the Universe are Durga,* Kali, Saraswati,* Lakshmi,* Parvati,* Sita, and Radha.

There are some temples and places of worship where great saints and spiritual teachers are revered and worshiped and others where only the symbol *Om* is worshiped. In some temples, the study of scriptures, meditation, and service to humanity are emphasized. In these temples, worship of the deities is done personally or in a small group.

Narayana: nah-RAH-ya-na
Nataraj: nat-RAHJ
Shivalingam: shi-va-LING-gam

Ganesha: ga-NEY-sha
Ramayana: rah-MAH-ya-na
Durga: DOOR-gah

Saraswati: sa-RUS-wah-ti
Lakshmi: LAHK-shmee
Parvati: PAHR-va-ti

Offering Worship

IN A TEMPLE, GOD IS PRESENT AS A LIVING BEING who receives our worship and love and who blesses us. The priest of the temple gives a ritual bath to the *murtis* with water, milk, and other sacred ingredients while reciting special prayers called *mantras*. This ceremony is called *abhishekam.** Then the priest adorns the *murtis* with sandalwood paste, *kumkum* (a red paste), and garlands of flowers.

We give the priest the offerings that we have brought with us. The priest will offer them to God while reciting *mantras* that say, "O God, please accept whatever has been offered to you by the devotees and bless them."

While the priest is offering, we stand in front of the shrine and bow to God to show our highest respect and humility. There are three kinds of salutations, or bows. The first and simplest salutation is called *ekanga pranam,** in which we simply fold our palms and bow down our heads. The second salutation is called *panchanga** pranam*, in which our knees, elbows, and head touch the ground. The third is called *sashtanga** pranam*, in which we lie face down with our arms stretched in prayer position. During salutations, we recite *mantras* or pray silently. We pray to God for knowledge and devotion. We also pray for the well-being of family members, friends, and all people.

After making the offering, the priest may bring to us the offered water, which we sip from our right palm. If the priest brings offered sandal-wood paste or *kumkum*, then we wear it on our forehead. This mark on the fore-head is called *tilak** and helps us to focus our minds on God.

When the priest brings the offered fruits, coconuts, or sweets blessed by God, we share them with our family and friends. The fruits and food we bring to the temple for offering are called *naivedyam.** After they are offered

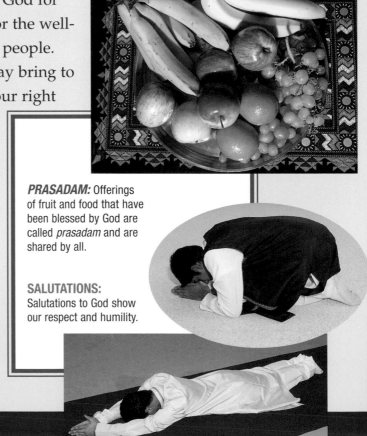

PRASADAM: Offerings of fruit and food that have been blessed by God are called *prasadam* and are shared by all.

SALUTATIONS: Salutations to God show our respect and humility.

and then blessed by God, they are called *prasadam*.* Hindus believe that eating *prasadam* nourishes the minds of devotees and helps to develop good thoughts and love for God.

At the end of our visit to the temple, we walk around the shrine in a clockwise direction, repeating God's name. This is called *pradakshina*. The idea is to make God the center of our lives, as we do in the *pradakshina*. By circling in a clockwise direction, we always keep God on our right side.

Before leaving the temple we sit quietly and do *japa*, repeating the names of God. *Japa* done in a holy place helps develop love for God.

Abhishekam: a-bee-SHEY-kam   *Panchanga:* pun-CHANG   *Naivedyam:* nay-VEH-dyam
Ekanga pranam: *Sashtanga:* sahs-TANG   *Prasadam:* pra-SAH-dam
   E-kang pra-NAHM   *Tilak:* tee-LUK

Arati and *Kirtan*

ARATI* IS A SPECIAL WORSHIP in which the priest offers to God a lamp with five or seven lighted wicks, circling it around the *murti* in a clockwise direction while ringing a bell. The lamp lights up God's beautiful face, which is very pleasing to the eyes of the devotees. *Arati* also includes offerings of incense and food, a fan,

ARATI LAMP: The special *arati* lamp has five or seven lights.

and other items of worship. *Arati* is accompanied by singing, the ringing of bells, and the playing of musical instruments. Some temples have a special *arati* at a fixed time in the morning and evening. People love to attend the *arati*. They join in singing, sometimes clapping their hands. After *arati*, the priest brings the lighted lamp to us. We receive the blessed light by putting our palms over the lamp and then by gently touching our palms to our eyes and our forehead. Devotees donate money in the plate of *arati* or in the donation box in the temple. The donations are used to pay the temple's regular expenses and are also given to the needy.

Singing the names and praises of God is called *kirtan.** It is usually done in a group. One person or a group of people leads the singing, and others repeat the words after them. *Kirtan* helps to focus our minds on developing love of God. In many temples, *kirtan* is a part of the regular services.

KIRTAN: Musical instruments such as drums, flutes, and *veenas* are used in *kirtan*.

Kirtan is made up of three kinds of singing: *dhuns,** *bhajans,** and *stotras** (or hymns). A one-line *mantra* or a line consisting of God's name chanted again and again in various melodies is called a *dhun*. Songs written by saints or devotees describing the glories of God are called *bhajans*. Many *bhajans* and *stotras* are poems based on the scriptures. *Stotras* are written in Sanskrit by great spiritual teachers and have been preserved and recited by millions of people over thousands of years.

Arati: AR-a-tee
Kirtan: KEER-tan
Dhuns: doons
Bhajans: bah-JANS
Stotras: STO-tras

Performing *Puja*

WHEN A SPECIAL GUEST COMES TO A HINDU HOME, we greet the guest with love and offer the very best of whatever we have. We give him or her the most comfortable seat, offer the tastiest drink, and serve the finest food to eat. We also give the best gift we can afford.

Similarly, in a Hindu worship of God called *puja*,* devotees receive God with love and respect using the holiest articles of worship. A special brass or copper pot called a *kalasha* or *purna kumbha** is filled with sacred water and kept in the front of the altar. In the pot, a few banana leaves are arranged and a coconut is placed on top of the leaves. Sometimes a red or white thread or a red cloth is tied around the pot. The *kalasha* represents the divine life force.

KALASHA:
The special pot
kept in front of the altar.

CONCH SHELL: A conch shell used
on the altar is dabbed with red
kumkum and sandalwood paste.

Conch shells are blown before the beginning of worship and during *arati* to signify the sound of *Om*. A special conch shell filled with water is also used in the worship. Rice, barley, *kusha* grass, sandalwood paste, *kumkum*, and other articles are combined to make an *arghya** offering to welcome God.

This *puja* is done in our homes or in a temple with five, ten, or sixteen special articles. We always include sandalwood paste, flowers, incense, a lamp, and a food offering. Holy *Ganga* water from the Ganges River in India is used to purify all the articles. Worship in the temple may include a *homa* ritual, in which the devotees make their offering to God in the form of a sacred fire.

In another *puja*, called *manasa puja* (worship in the mind), we use things from nature as *puja* articles. In *manasa puja*, the heart is a seat for God; the sun, moon, and stars are the light of the lamp of the *arati*; the wind is a fan; the sound of *Om* is a bell, and fruits

Puja: POO-jah   *Purna kumbha:* POOR-na KOOM-bah   *Arghya:* AR-a-gya

and flowers are *naivedyam*. At the end of *manasa puja*, flowers representing virtues such as compassion, knowledge, forgiveness, truth, non-violence, and honesty are offered at the feet of God.

GIVING OUR BEST: Our finest foods are offered to God as the honored guest in the temple.

Learning through Scriptures

READING SCRIPTURES and listening to explanations of scriptures are important activities in a Hindu temple. Occasionally a holy person or a scholar is invited to talk about the scriptures.

The Sanskrit word *veda* means knowledge. Vedas are the holy books of the Hindus. There are four Vedas: Rig Veda, Yajur* Veda, Atharva* Veda, and Sama Veda. Vedas are the oldest books on earth and are the foundation of Hindu philosophy and religion. *Rishis* are sages, or holy men, who have seen God. Vedas are collections of their experiences of God. Vedas teach the ways of worship and proper behavior. Vedic chanting is the reciting of Sanskrit verses from the Vedas. It is inspiring and spiritually uplifting.

The Upanishads are holy writings from the Vedas that are the foundation of Hindu philosophy. The Bhagavad Gita shows us how to practice the teachings of Upanishads in our daily life. In some temples devotees recite all the seven hundred verses of the Bhagavad Gita on special occasions.

RAMAYANA: The *Ramayana* is a long poem originally written in Sanskrit, the ancient language of India.

SCRIPTURES: Study of the Hindu scriptures is an important part of young people's education.

Hindu philosophy has also been explained through stories and legends collected in the eighteen Puranas—collections of stories glorifying the virtues and powers of the gods and goddesses—and through the two great poems, the *Ramayana* and the *Mahabharata.** The *Ramayana* and *Mahabharata* strongly influence the daily lives of Hindus. Some temples arrange recitations of the *Ramayana,* in which the stories are retold to large congregations, often through music and dance and always with great devotion.

The Vedas and the Upanishads have been translated from Sanskrit into many languages of the world. The Hindu scriptures have also been made available in storybooks so that children can learn about the scriptures and understand their rich cultural heritage. Children love to read these exciting illustrated stories, which bring to life the many forms of God.

When we go to a temple, we may find classes for children to learn Sanskrit, Vedic chanting, and Hindu scriptures. Many temples also have a bookstore and a library where people can obtain scriptures and other inspiring books.

Yajur: ya-JOOR   Atharva: a-THAR-va   *Mahabharata:* ma-HAH-BAH-ra-ta

Reaching Out to Community

A HINDU TEMPLE is a religious, social, cultural, educational, and spiritual center. Hindus believe that serving all human beings is the same as serving God. A popular verse says, "Let me tell you the essence of all the scriptures in half a verse: To help others is a merit and to harm others is a sin."

Temple organizers collect donations to help the needy people of the community. During times of natural disasters such as floods or earthquakes, temples make special efforts to raise funds to help the people in that area. In some houses of worship, young people are encouraged to conduct food drives regularly to help the poor.

Some temples have weekend classes for young people as a service to the community. In these classes, students learn important values, inspiring stories, biographies of great people, scriptures, Sanskrit, *kirtan*, and chanting. Students are also encouraged to volunteer in local programs that feed the hungry, nursing homes, and hospitals.

Some temples also offer classes to learn the regional Indian languages and classical music and dance. Many temples have an auditorium where special lectures and religious activities are held.

CHANT: Girls and boys sit comfortably on the floor in traditional chanting position.

SANSKRIT: Children practice writing the shapes of Sanskrit letters in weekend classes.

Celebrations and Festivals

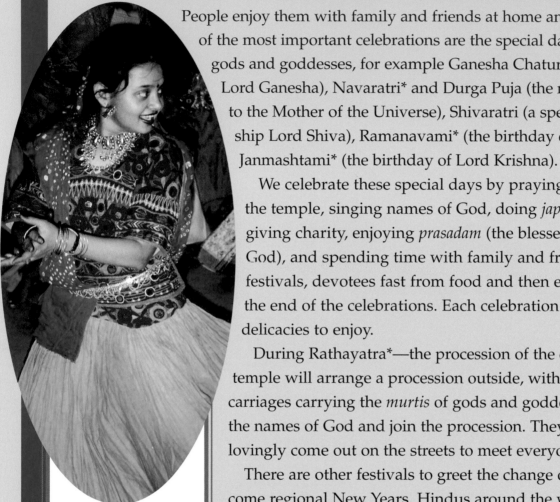

CELEBRATING: People enjoy the festivals that occur throughout the year. They wear traditional Indian clothing and jewelry, and they anoint their foreheads with sandalwood or red *kumkum* paste.

THERE ARE MANY HINDU CELEBRATIONS AND FESTIVALS held throughout the year. People enjoy them with family and friends at home and in the temple. Some of the most important celebrations are the special days associated with gods and goddesses, for example Ganesha Chaturthi* (the birthday of Lord Ganesha), Navaratri* and Durga Puja (the nine nights dedicated to the Mother of the Universe), Shivaratri (a special evening to worship Lord Shiva), Ramanavami* (the birthday of Lord Rama), and Janmashtami* (the birthday of Lord Krishna).

We celebrate these special days by praying at home, going to the temple, singing names of God, doing *japa* and meditating, giving charity, enjoying *prasadam* (the blessed food offered to God), and spending time with family and friends. During some festivals, devotees fast from food and then enjoy a great feast at the end of the celebrations. Each celebration has special kinds of delicacies to enjoy.

During Rathayatra*—the procession of the chariot of God—a temple will arrange a procession outside, with beautifully decorated carriages carrying the *murtis* of gods and goddesses. Devotees chant the names of God and join the procession. They feel as if God has lovingly come out on the streets to meet everyone in person.

There are other festivals to greet the change of seasons and to welcome regional New Years. Hindus around the world regard India as their holy place, so to continue the traditions they celebrate Indian festivals wherever they live. Major celebrations include Diwali* (the festival of light), Makar Sankranti* (the festival related to the sun), Holi (the festival of colors), Baishakhi* and Vishu* (spring harvest festivals), Gudhi Padawa* and Yugadi (summer festivals), Raksha Bandhan (Sister's day and the festival of friendship and unity), and Onam (the fall harvest festival). See the last page of this book for a list of when these celebrations take place.

VISHU: A beautiful home altar displays fruits and flowers for the spring harvest festival called Vishu. On the morning of Vishu, a child, covering his or her own eyes, is led to the altar by the mother. On this lucky day, the first thing the child is supposed to see is the beautiful face of God and feel God's blessings in the bountiful harvest.

Chaturthi: cha-TUR-thee
Navaratri: na-va-RAH-tree
Ramanavami: RAHM-na-va-mee
Janmashtami: jan-MAHST-mee

Rathayatra: ra-tha-YAH-tra
Diwali: dee-WAH-lee
Makar Sankranti:
   MAH-ker san-KRAN-tee

Baishkhi: bay-SHA-kee
Vishu: vee-SHOO
Gudhi Padawa:
   goo-DEE PAD-wa

Diwali, the Festival of Light

DIWALI IS A MAJOR HINDU FESTIVAL. During Diwali, the goddesses Kali, Saraswati, and Lakshmi are worshiped, in addition to the other forms of God. Diwali also celebrates Lord Rama's victory over the demon Ravana and Rama's return to his kingdom of Ayodhya.

In India there is a Diwali holiday that lasts for seven to ten days. To celebrate Diwali in America, we take one or two days off from school and work. We visit relatives and friends and enjoy delicious meals together.

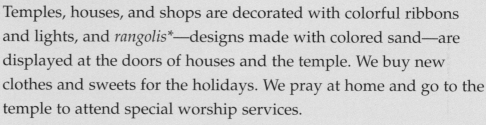

RANGOLIS: *Rangolis* are made with colored sand to decorate doorways of temples and houses.

Temples, houses, and shops are decorated with colorful ribbons and lights, and *rangolis**—designs made with colored sand—are displayed at the doors of houses and the temple. We buy new clothes and sweets for the holidays. We pray at home and go to the temple to attend special worship services.

In the temple, gods and goddesses are adorned with new clothes and garlands of flowers and colorful ribbons. Devotees prepare vegetable dishes and sweets and offer them to God. The temple priests artfully arrange all these dishes in front of the image of God. This display of delicacies is called *annakuta*.* After the display, all the dishes are distributed to the devotees as *prasadam*.

Diwali is also a festival of lights. At night, the shrines in the houses and the temple are decorated with lighted lamps. At home, people light lamps made out of earthen pots and arrange them near the doors around the colorful designs of *rangoli*. A lamp is a symbol of knowledge because it destroys the darkness and lights

ANNAKUTA: Each festival has delicious foods that are offered to God and then shared with devotees.

our path; it is a symbol of love because it gives warmth; and it is a symbol of purity because it burns away our bad thoughts. At night, people go to the temple to attend evening *arati* and to see fireworks. In India, children enjoy fireworks at their homes under the supervision of parents.

Rangolis: run-GO-lees   *Annakuta:* AN-NA-koot

FESTIVAL OF LIGHTS:
Shrines in temples and homes are decorated with lighted lamps made of earthen pots.

SPIRITUAL TEACHERS: Photographs of the great nineteenth- and twentieth-century spiritual teachers Sri Ramakrishna *(top),* his wife Sri Sarada Devi *(right),* and Swami Vivekananda *(left)* are an honored part of this altar along with Lord Shiva *(center).*

Honoring Our Teachers

OTHER SPECIAL DAYS ARE CELEBRATED when Hindus pay the highest honor to their spiritual teachers, who are considered to be prophets, saints, and even human forms of God. We celebrate a special day called Guru Purnima* for all spiritual teachers and we also celebrate days in honor of Buddha, Mahavira, Shankaracharya, Ramanuja, Shri Chaitanya,* Shri Swaminarayan, Guru Nanak, Sri Ramakrishna,* Sri Sarada Devi,* Andal, and other great teachers.

We observe these special days at home and in the temple. On these days, we think and talk about the lives and wisdom of these great teachers, and prayers are offered to them. Some of these saints were great poets, and their devotional songs are still sung today. The birthday of a great prophet, Swami Vivekananda,* is celebrated as a "youth day" in India and America with events such as speech and essay competitions and activities organized to help the needy.

Some temples hold a graduation ceremony for students who have completed their religious studies. A graduation sermon from the Upanishad is recited. It provides clear guidelines for the future lives of these students.

LORD MAHAVIRA: People pray and meditate before the images of great spiritual teachers such as Lord Mahavira.

Purnima: POOR-nee-ma
Shri Chaitanya: SHREE chay-TAN-ya
Sri Ramakrishna: SREE RAHM-krish-na
Sri Sarada Devi: SREE SAHR-a-da DE-vee
Vivekananda: vi-VE-kah-nan-da

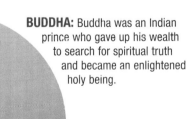

BUDDHA: Buddha was an Indian prince who gave up his wealth to search for spiritual truth and became an enlightened holy being.

Blessings throughout Our Lives

HINDUS DIVIDE A PERSON'S LIFE INTO FOUR MAIN STAGES: that of a student, that of a family man or woman, that of a retired person, and that of one leading a dedicated life. Student life focuses on education and self-development. Family life emphasizes earning a living and taking care of family and social responsibilities. Retired life stresses spiritual development. Dedicated life emphasizes focusing the mind on God and serving all beings as if they were also God. There are rituals that celebrate each stage of life and ask for the blessings of God at that stage. These rituals are called *samskaras*.*

VIDYARAMBHA: To celebrate the beginning of a child's education, parents help children write *"Om"* on a plate filled with rice grains.

Namakarana* is done for a new baby. Prayers are offered at home or at a temple, and the name of the child is whispered in his or her ear by a priest or by the father of the child.

Annaprasana* celebrates the child receiving God's blessings when cooked grains are given to the child to eat for the first time. At that time, prayers are offered at home or at a temple for the child's nourishment and growth.

The Vidyarambha* celebrates the beginning of the child's education. On or before the child's first day of school, the family asks Lord Ganesha and Goddess Saraswati for their blessings for the child to excel in studies. The child is guided by parents to write *Om* and letters on a plate filled with rice grains.

UPANAYANA: In the Upanayana ceremony, the priest gives the boys a sacred thread to keep them mindful of prayer and worship of God.

The Upanayana* and Initiation *samskaras* occur as children grow older, between ages nine and fifteen. Traditionally, boys are given a sacred thread to initiate them into prayers, worship of God, and study of the scriptures. They are also given a holy *mantra,* called the Gayatri* mantra, to repeat daily. In modern times, Initiation by spiritual teachers can be given to both boys and girls. In this ceremony, a boy or girl is initiated to pray to God for knowledge, devotion, and spiritual development. A *mantra* is given to the child to repeat daily to focus the mind on God.

Vivaha* is the marriage ceremony performed in a temple or in a wedding hall by a priest. A fire-offering ritual called *homa* is performed, and marriage vows are taken in

VIVAHA: The bridal couple walks around the sacred fire *(homa)* in their wedding ceremony.

the presence of the sacred fire. Then, the bride and the bridegroom worship the sacred fire as their first religious act as a couple. They are encouraged to fulfill five kinds of responsibilities during their family life to the best of their ability. These responsibilities are daily prayers, daily scriptural studies, living a virtuous life, serving human beings with respect and love, and taking care of the environment.

Samskaras: sams-KAH-rahs
Namakarana: NAHM-ka-ran-a
Annaprasana: an-na-PRAH-san-na

Vidyarambha: vid-ya-RAM-bah
Upanayana: U-PAH-nay-na
Gayatri: GAH-ya-tri

Vivaha: vee-WAH

The Heart of the Family

FAMILY SHRINE: A Hindu family brings a picture of an image of God to live in their new home.

THE HINDU RELIGION TEACHES that each person must try to grow spiritually. For this reason, almost all Hindu homes have a small family shrine. Before the family moves to a new residence, an image of God (a *murti,* where God comes to live) or a picture of an image of God is brought into the house with honor and respect and placed in a family shrine.

The shrine is the heart of the family. Every day, in the morning and evening, family members offer to God a lighted lamp, incense, and prayers. On special occasions, such as birthdays, wedding anniversaries, the first day of school or of a new job, and on religious holidays, the family decorates the shrine with flowers and lights. On some occasions, they invite close relatives and friends to their home and offer prayers and various delicacies to God and enjoy the blessed food as *prasadam.*

The family shrine provides peace and comfort in sad times and adds joy in happy times. We know that God is always with us, everywhere.

Here are a few prayers we recite in Hindu temples and homes:

Let me hear, O God, the words that are good and sweet.
Let me see the beautiful things that fill my heart with joy.
Let me have a strong body, to sing thy glories and devote my life to your work.

O God, you are my mother, you are my father, you are my sibling, and you are my friend.
You are my knowledge, and you are my wealth. You are my all in all.

May all attain happiness. May all be healthy. May all seek beneficial goals. May no one suffer. Om Peace, Peace, Peace be unto all living beings.

SHRI SWAMINARAYAN MANDIR
BAPS Swaminarayan Sanstha
Houston, Texas

SRI SATYANARAYANA TEMPLE
Connecticut Valley Hindu Temple Society
Middletown, Connecticut

SRI VENKATESWARA TEMPLE (BALAGI MANDIR) AND COMMUNITY CENTER
Hindu Temple and Cultural Society of USA
Bridgewater, New Jersey

Hindu Temples in North America

HINDU TEMPLES ARE FOUND ALL OVER THE WORLD. Since Hindus believe that God is one but has many forms, various Hindu temples worship various forms of God.

However, all Hindu temples teach us to build a temple in our own hearts. If we develop virtues and establish God in our hearts, then we become living temples. As a result, people around us feel God's presence in our thoughts, speech, and actions. Finally, temples teach us to love and serve all beings as if they were the Living God.

Namaste. Visit us again!

Hindu Religious Celebrations & Festivals

Hindu religious celebrations and festivals are based mostly on the lunar (moon) calendar, which is different from the solar (sun) calendar used in North America. The following is a list of major Hindu celebrations and festivals along with the months in which they take place.

January
Swami Vivekananda's Birthday (Youth Day)
Makar Sankranti

February/March
Shivaratri
Sri Ramakrishna's Birthday
Holi
Shri Chaitanya's Birthday

March/April
Yugadi / Gudhi Padawa
Ramanavami
Lord Mahavir's Birthday
Shri Swaminarayan's Birthday

April
Vishu
Baishakhi

May/June
Shri Ramanuja's Birthday
Shri Shankaracharya's Birthday
Lord Buddha's Birthday

June/July
Rathayatra

July
Guru Purnima

August/September
Raksha Bandhan
Janmashtami
Ganesha Chaturthi
Onam

September/October
Navaratri
Durga Puja

October/November
Diwali

November/December
Gita Jayanti
Guru Nanak's Birthday

December/January
Holy Mother Sri Sarada Devi's Birthday